MW01516353

POWERHOUSE WEBSITES

IMPROVE YOUR WEBSITE TO 10X YOUR BRANDING, PROFITS, AND BUSINESS

ALLEN ASHOURI

EMRG

11601 Wilshire Blvd. 5th Floor
Los Angeles, CA 90025
(310) 747-4282
info@emrgonline.com

Editor: Joshua Myles Halimi
Designer & Jr. Editor: Michael J. Shymanski

Printed in the United States of America.

CONTENTS

PREFACE:
THIS BOOK'S ULTIMATE GOAL

I hope that through reading this book you learn about the best practices all websites should include at this point in time. The reason I say this point in time is because there are constantly new technologies and new improvements being developed. What worked 10 years ago is not as effective today, nor will what is being used today be as effective 10 years from now.

Knowing that websites are evolving, you will gain a fundamental understanding from this book to structure your thought process on websites as new techniques emerge. What took me 20+ years of working with hundreds of clients is in this book to help you learn it in a much easier fashion, and in much less time. I'll share some of my client website projects, and the different things my company learned from them; lessons in both websites and business. Understanding both of these trains of thought will help you immensely on your journey. It definitely has for us, as we went from a team of 1, to a team of over 50. From 1 client, to hundreds of clients. From small businesses and mom-and-pops to international multi-billion dollar Fortune 50 clients. I'll open up my secret notes that I've accumulated over the last 20 years and share them with you all in hopes that they'll be helpful for you on your journey.

You won't become a website developer, coder, or programmer. That's not the purpose of this book. You will, however, get a fundamental understanding of what every website needs to run, what elements take a website from good to great, and the utility you can gain from a strong conversion-focused website to help you grow your business/organization. We'll start with the basics—getting a domain name, understanding hosting, and security. We will then take a deep dive into strategies, branding, design, development, and the profitability/results a great website can give you.

Whether you're an e-commerce business, medical practice, legal firm, non-profit, insurance company, real estate developer or operator, or sell strawberry jam from your garage—every business can gain immensely from a strong website. A well-performing website can streamline your operations. You can multiply your revenues and profits 100 times over. You can leverage technology for almost any purpose. You can make your life easier, and scale your company larger than you ever imagined. Picture having a store that sells electronics. You are limited by how many people you have running the register, how much local marketing you're able to successfully run, and a million other limitations. Now picture having an e-commerce business. Your website sells electronics online and can sell to an unlimited number of people at one time. Your website can be marketed around the world and has far fewer limitations (if any). While this might be unique to e-commerce businesses, each business type has many advantageous opportunities through a website if the right technology is deployed.

Here's a perfect example of what a good website can help you do. This is a recent situation with one of my clients: she has a storefront business that sells high-end furniture. Best of all, she's killing it. Her numbers are growing year by year, and the business is extremely profitable. But, she was constantly bogged down with dealing with customers, opening the store on time, managing her showroom employees, and all that goes into operating a store. As a previous store owner myself, I felt her pain and knew exactly what she was dealing with. But what if there was another way?

She and I have had discussions in the past about moving towards an e-commerce business model for a while now. We had even tested and successfully ran some ads on the new e-commerce website we had built for her. Yes, there were definitely challenges at first, especially with shipping these large items. But we worked through them. We figured out solutions and started selling more of her inventory online. Over the course of the last year, she has moved from doing less than 10% of her total sales online, to the majority of her sales being online! Even better, she's more profitable than she was before! The cherry on top—she is working less than ever before: less time managing employees, less time with customers, less time dealing with running a storefront. You can do the same for yourself.

Let's take a quick journey together and see how you can change your business and your life through your website.

INTRO

I started my first company as a teenager. I kind of fell into it. I was taking a computer skills class when a neighbor overheard me talking with my mom about what I had learned, and asked me for some help. Margaret. Such a nice older woman; in her mid-80s and eager to learn more about how email works (this is back in 2002). Her apartment was a few floors above ours, and I had seen her around the building. I remember the first time I walked into her apartment. She had awards and pictures all over her walls; I had no idea Margaret had such a strong professional background. Her computer was sitting on her old wooden desk with two chairs ready for us. Her papers were perfectly organized, and her notepad and pencil were ready to go. This is how my journey started.

Margaret was an organized and fair person. She knew what she wanted, and was assertive in getting it; she was determined to learn about computers, how emails work, and how to get better at typing. So, she made me an offer: $10/hr for a minimum of 10 hours. Not bad for a 12 year old kid in 2002 (minimum wage was about $6.75 at the time). What turned out to be more important than the money was the lesson I learned—she taught me the value in sharing my knowledge with others, and how there was a big need for people to keep up with technology. Who knew a business was going to emerge from this one-off situation-turned-transaction.

I didn't know much about computers, just enough to help her very basic needs. What I did know was that I LOVED feeling independent. I loved the idea of making my own money, especially at the age of 12. This quickly made me learn that I loved business too. The concept of barter stood out to me; someone needed something and I was able to provide it to them in exchange for money. What a concept! This is how it all started. There was a need/pain in the market, and I wanted to provide the solution.

Over the years, I got a lot of practice and experience in business. I remember putting up fliers to attract new customers; it started with my apartment complex, grew to my neighborhood, and later on to targeted neighborhoods. I remember raising my prices for the first time, and learning to actually ask for payments. A few times early on I was too shy and just left after providing the service. I even remember my first hire. I was 16, and he was 45. I wore the nicest suit I had and had sunglasses on to hide my clean-shaved face that made me look even younger. I really wanted him to like me. I remember the fear and intimidation, the wonder of "how will I possibly get this guy to respect and listen to me?"

When you're a punk kid just trying to be a "professional," dealing with someone much older and more experienced is intimidating. But through my time working on my business I had to go through the hiring process countless times. Little did I know that I would have to go through this obstacle many times, and slowly gain confidence through experience and repetition.

Fast forward 10 years later and I had a computer store. I loved helping my clients. Customer service came naturally to me because it was part of help-ing people—something I've always enjoyed doing. Sometimes this led me to unchartered territories though. We were a computer repair shop, but my clients needed more. They would ask me to come on-site to their homes—so I did. They asked me to come on-site to their businesses—so I did. They asked me to help build them a website—so I learned how, and then I did.

Little did I know that there was a much BIGGER lesson here than I might have understood at the time:

LISTEN TO YOUR CUSTOMERS' NEEDS.

I thought I was jumping around and just trying to hustle. But there was more to it. After all, they were MY customers. They needed help. Another pain, another opportunity for another solution. This is getting interesting...

CHAPTER 1

BUILDING A WEBSITE - THE BASICS

This was a new journey for me. What did I know about websites? Nothing at the time. But I knew people who had websites. I started asking them questions and learning how they built theirs. I knew there were platforms where I could hire people to build a website. So, I started messaging people, hiring, and learning the process. I started piecing together what things were needed to go from start-to-finish. At the time it felt like gibberish. There are so many technical terms, it almost felt like a different language. Once you start understanding it with logic though, it's a lot easier to digest. Let's run through this together.

1. Domain Registration - Every website has a domain name, also known as URL (i.e. www.EMRGonline.com). In order to register a domain, you pay a website like GoDaddy.com $15 or so a year to own the rights to that name. Try it out. Go to GoDaddy.com, type in a website name, and if it's available you'll see you can register/buy it for one or more years. When that time expires, you'll have the first right to renew before anyone else.

A few strategies to keep in mind when registering a domain so you can make the most out of it:

- If you have your company name already, try to get it as close as possible based on what's available.

- If you have a long company name, you might want a logical shortening of your name. None of your clients will enjoy typing in a 500 character website to reach your site. 😆

- If you're establishing a new company brand/name, don't limit yourself. Think of future growth. I could have called our company EMRG Websites, but I anticipated that we would grow into different digital marketing service lines. I saved myself a headache.

2. Build the Website - We'll go into details later, but for the sake of this portion of this book I want you to understand that a website is a collection of codes and files that make it look (design) and act (functionality) the way it does. Take a look at our site below as an example.

The colors, fonts, images, icons, pages, functions and EVERYTHING else you see is a result of a combination of dev codes and files formatted in a specific way. With today's tech, possibilities are endless for what functions can be created: e-commerce, user logins, uploading files, livechat, video conferencing...

Start thinking about how your business operates. What functions can you potentially have your website do to offload work for yourself or your employees? If you're a medical practice, this can include new patient forms. For legal firms, think of qualifying questions for new clients that you might put on a website form rather than having your intake team (or even one of your lawyers) obtain on a lengthy phone call. Start putting all these ideas down in your notes. (This will help us in a bit.)

To make it easier, we've created a free guide that you can use to start storing your notes with some structured guidance: www.EMRGonline.com/Powerhouse-Websites/website-wishlist

I suggest you use this free tool since the next steps will build on it.

3. Hosting - Assuming that you have registered the domain name and built your website through a combination of codes and files, you now need somewhere to "host" these codes and files, connecting your website to the internet for people to access when they type in your website name. If you think about it logically, it makes sense. You have all these codes and files that make up your website, but if they are just on your computer how can anyone see them? They need to be HOSTED somewhere where it connects to the internet for all to see!

Hosting comes in all shapes and sizes, from $10/month to thousands per month. It depends on a number of factors: from website file size, to functionality, to how many users are on your site at any given time, security, and the types of files that your site hosts. I've seen a lot of websites get hacked because their managers decided to use the "cheaper" hosting solutions. Ironically, this turned out to be much more expensive for them to fix or restore (when possible) after being hacked or having the site go down. Many didn't have back-ups and were forced to hire us to rebuild an entirely new website. This unlucky group was much more eager to have us host their new websites after tasting how bad it can get. I suggest going with something mid-tier at a minimum. Go with a company you trust who will respond relatively quickly without you having to be on hold for customer service for days. Save yourself the agony.

Hosting speed is important too, especially if you have a large website with many users or if there is some functionality on the site. For example, if you run an e-commerce business that strictly sells online, the website must have a lot of functionality in order to perform the transactions, inventory management, etc. Therefore, the server that your website is hosted on should be high performing in order to avoid your website slowing down. So if you have an e-commerce business, you should invest in some strong hosting. This is your entire business model! Imagine if you went on Amazon.com and it took 45 seconds to load each time. Or if you timed out when trying to buy something. Don't deter your customers.

4. Security - This is a big unknown for most, but it's vital to keep you safe. Whenever you have a website (especially if you're processing transactions on it, or storing sensitive info—like payment or customer details), you should have a SSL certificate installed on your website. SSL stands for "secure socket layer," but that's not important. What's important is that you understand that this encrypts the connection between your website and the people on it, acting like a security system for your website.

SSLs also come in all shapes and sizes. Depending on how much sensitive info you have and the nature of your business and website, you might need a stronger SSL to keep you safe.

5. Back-Ups - Do yourself a favor: the minute your website is live, set up a recurring back-up system on your website!

Scenario 1 - You don't back-up your website. Your website crashes and all that hard work you put in is lost! You realize, "I have to start from scratch!" Now you feel like jumping off a bridge.

Scenario 2 - You take an immediate back-up right after you launch your website. Great! You are safe! Well, kind of. Two years down the road your website crashes. But in the past two years you completely changed the content on your website. Your images were updated three months ago. Hell, you probably added way more functionality and design to the site. But your back-up only gives you the older version of the site, which doesn't even make sense for your business anymore. Does that mean I have to rebuild a majority of this website, or is it better to start from scratch at this point? Where's that bridge…

Scenario 3 - I listened to Allen and got a daily back-up system. My site crashed! No problem, let's get that bad boy restored. But it's been a year and we added thousands of new products, pages, content, team member bios, design, functionality, SEO, etc. No problem, let's get that bad boy restored. Your business never skips a beat.

If you need help with a domain name, hosting, or any of the steps above, send us an email at <u>info@EMRGonline.com</u>. We'll see what your website goals entail and get you on your journey.

That's about it for the basics. Not that hard, right? Let's take a deeper dive.

CHAPTER 2
FINALIZING WEBSITE
GOALS & OBJECTIVES

"Knowing where you want to go before departing on your journey will help you arrive at the correct destination."

—I came up with that bad boy myself.

I'll never forget one of my first website clients. He was a tough SOB. A lawyer with a reputation of being a fighter both in and out of court, go figure. Don't get me wrong, some of my best friends are lawyers. He wasn't a bad guy either, but he was very direct, very authoritative, and very intimidating to a young business owner with not a ton of experience. Plus, he was extremely demanding in any of the previous non-website work he had asked of me in the past, so I knew it would be hard to please him. I had to figure out the best way to do this. So, time for some research again.

I started looking up what the best processes were for building a website. Most of what I read online said to use templates for the easiest process. We agreed on a pre-built website, where I could just swap out the content on the site to what was unique to my client. Sounds great! I figured it out already—it's almost too good to be true. Right...

Templates can come with a lot of their own issues. In this case it wasn't compatible with several web browsers, nor the platform the client wanted. But what do I do now? He already approved the design. I already spent half my budget building out this template. I couldn't go back to him now. I had to figure out a way to build this...

Fast forward a month, many all-nighters, and 10x as many hours as I had expected to put into this project, and presto! I toughed it out and cus-tom-built the website I promised to without the template, with the design he approved, and both browser and platform compatibility. This will make even him happy, right?

I met with him one last time to showcase the site. I was so proud. I even told him of the hurdles we faced. I expressed how the template we chose wasn't compatible and that we had to rebuild the entire design from scratch to make it compatible. "Why would you do that? I didn't even care about the design that much." I'll never forget that moment. A dagger to the heart! I still remember that feeling of the deep pit in my stomach when I heard those words. All that hard work. Where did I go wrong?

In hindsight, I see my mistakes. Something I can share with each of you to avoid feeling left unhappy with your own website after it is built. There was a huge lesson in this that I would discover after a few dozen more websites:

START WITH THE END GOAL IN MIND.

This has been a very useful technique for me in my life as well as for all of my businesses. I teach this religiously to each of my employees as well as all the people I mentor. Knowing your exact end goal prior to any project is extremely effective. It gives you an exact target to go after and helps you hit success much more often. We did the same thing with this book when you first picked it up.

The first line of this book clearly states, "I hope that through reading this book you learn about the best practices all websites should include at this point in time." This gave both of us an exact objective before you started reading. You now know your goal and are much more likely to hit it when reading this book.

Back to the client. The reason he wasn't impressed with all that time I spent on that design was because that design wasn't important for him. What was important for him was to grow his business. In order to do that, he needed a professionally designed website for his law firm. There were many designs that could help him achieve that goal.

So, what are your goals? They might be to have a professional presence online. Maybe to validate your business as reputable, to showcase your past work. Maybe to show all your existing clients your other services lines that can be of value to them. Maybe you want to streamline your business operations by having people fill out forms, make purchases, or communicate with you directly through your website. Again with today's tech the possibilities are endless. But, it is vital that you write down exactly what you want to achieve by having a website. The more direct and clear you are about this, the higher your chance of being successful through the build of your website.

You might have a ton of goals. Great! Get them all down. Budget might require you to cut down on some of your goals, possibly building your site out over time. Sometimes timing is the limiting factor, requiring you to build out your dream website in phases rather than in one shot. Either way, write them all down. Then, prioritize them by putting them in order of importance, with the most important first. This is where an experienced digital consultant should help guide you on the best way to implement these ideas and include as many of them as possible given any constraints. Work together and finalize this. This will serve as your guiding compass for the rest of the project. Knowing where you want to go before departing on your journey will help you arrive at the correct destination.

You can continue to use our free tools here to help organize your notes. This will be helpful as we continue to build on our thoughts in future chapters: www.EMRGonline.com/Powerhouse-Websites/website-end-goals

CHAPTER 3
PLAN OF ACTION -
FUNCTIONS, PAGES, & SCOPE

Let's fast forward a few years. At this point in my career, I have hundreds of websites under my belt. My team is growing, most of my clients are very happy, and we're growing their businesses using our skills. Tony Robbins says, "Repetition is the mother of skill," and I'm feeling pretty skilled. I'm getting pretty good at this thing. I have the basics down and our designs are even starting to get recognized. But project budgets aren't being met. To be honest, they don't exist. This is a recipe for disaster with any type of project planning.

I can easily remember a dozen clients where we ended up going way over budget, but there was one particular client that sticks out. She was (and still is) a great human being. Super sweet, spiritual, and kind-hearted. She was a good friend of mine, and we even dated for a bit. Yeah, crossing boundaries all over the place. But that's not the lesson here, let's stay focused. Her business was growing rapidly, and we knew how we could help her make the most of it. She had a beautiful lifestyle brand that needed to be portrayed through her website better. Piece of cake! We knew what we had to do—for the most part. And she knew what she wanted—for the most part. Another item to go into our delicious recipe for disaster. Get your knife and fork ready...

As we built the site, we started getting revisions. We started getting additional requests. We even came up with a number of suggestions on how we can improve. In a nutshell, a two-month project ended up becoming a 6-month project with no end in sight and was costing us more than we were being paid. Even worse, it was affecting my friendship (and relationship) with the beautiful "her." How can she be so demanding and unreasonable? The funny thing is she was probably thinking to herself the same thing about us! I hated this feeling of anxiety; the feeling of disappointment from someone who hired my company, especially when the website was actually turning out to be pretty damn good. This anxiety pushed me to learn my lesson quickly. I'm sure there was something I could do to avoid this from ever happening again, and I was now driven to find out what this was.

As you move forward on building your own website, you are constantly going to think of new ideas that you want to add. Why wouldn't you? We mentioned the possibilities are endless, and if you have a tendency to want perfection like I naturally do (or are just very creative), then the rabbit hole can go deep. This is why it's imperative that you create a set scope of EXACTLY what you've decided to include based on your original "website wishlist" worksheet from the last chapter. Let's make sure we have that handy as we'll build on it for our next step. But how do you decide what stays and what doesn't? Let's prioritize with a quick exercise to help you get started.

Base Pages - These are pages every website should include:

1. Home - Display your branding with navigation options for people to find what they're looking for. Couple that with some quick

links or banner displays of your strongest message/service/product—this way, as soon as someone comes to your website, they are presented with one of your most popular options.

2. About - This page is an opportunity to talk about your company, history, team, and mission. Clients are looking more at your "why" than ever before, especially with so many options to choose from. By writing content that's specific, unique to your business (your *Value Proposition*), and explains why you exist, you'll attract the right type of clients who believe in your mission. This can make the biggest impact on how successful you will be.

3. Contact - This is a standard page most people are familiar with. It's important because people will intuitively know that they can get your contact information or submit a contact form directly on this page. If this is a potential client, you obviously want them to be able to connect with you as easily as possible. This is an easy way to obtain a **conversion**: when website traffic takes an action that you want them to and becomes a prospect. Web Traffic —› Prospect = Conversion.

4. Products/Services - In some unique cases, businesses will elect not to have this displayed. Though for the large majority, it's smart to list out your service offerings or products. If you are a cosmetic surgeon, you likely do more than just breast implants. You might also perform rhinoplasties, facelifts, or head transplants (apparently that's a thing). The last thing you want to do is alienate a potential head transplant patient by having your hands full with a breast implants-only website (pun intended). Or even worse, imagine both of these types of patients coming to your site but leaving before calling or filling out a form because they weren't sure you offered what they were looking for. You want them to feel comfortable working with you and to know that you specialize in both head and breasts! List them all out on your website.

Now that we have the basics, let's get specific. Let's use the following exercise to help you prioritize:

SCOPE

You've already got your basics (Home, About, Contact, and Services/Products), so let's dig deeper. What are other pages you need for your site to reach your goals?

Using the table, we are going to write the name of the page, a brief 1-2 sentence description, any functionalities, and how it helps you realize your goals.

We recommend referring to your website goals a few times, so you can work with them fresh in mind.

Use the following table at the link to continue with the exercise:
www.EMRGonline.com/Powerhouse-Websites/scope-of-work

Page Name	Description	Functionality (if any)	How will this help you reach your end goal?

By having this all laid out visibly you're able to see where you are headed. BUT, and this is a big but, you might not be able to include EVERYTHING that your dream website wishlist includes. This is why we need to prioritize. As I mentioned earlier, budget, time, and a number of other factors can limit what's feasible off the bat. Just like in life, we're forced to compromise and prioritize. Ah, another hidden gem life lesson during your website build.

Based on what's feasible, you choose as many as you can and you put the rest on hold. That's how life and business work. Don't beat yourself up as this is normal. We do the best we can with what we're able to and possibly get the rest done later. Think of the alternative of having nothing—this is definitely a much better option.

Amazing! You are now well on your way to building an incredible website for your business and possibly transforming your business. You've developed your blueprint. This is your treasure map to your end goal. This is your yellow brick road, Dorothy. This will help you avoid the fly-ing monkeys (or the mistakes I made earlier in my career).

STICK TO YOUR PLAN!

Don't mess it up with the pretty "her" (or "him"). Don't get frustrated and overwhelmed, fall behind on schedule, or get mad at yourself—all because you're constantly changing the expectations you set for yourself. You made a plan, now you have to execute it.

It is absolutely okay to want more and to be creative. It's even encouraged. Some of the best ideas will come about during your build, or even after (once you've seen user behavior on your website). You'll easily be able to tell once you see how it works for people and you see their feedback. But to ensure success, just write down all the other ideas that come to mind. Get this MVP (minimal viable product) live first, then keep building and adding to it. This way, your business can operate and go live ASAP. You can continuously improve your website AFTER going live (and possibly start to generate new revenue or streamline your operations through your website). Trust me, once you see how much this can benefit your business, you will continue to build and evolve your website to help you even more.

"Perfection is the enemy of progress."

—Winston Churchill

Why wouldn't you? People are looking to use technology and websites much more than ever. And, you can bet your ass that our society is only going to become more heavily reliant on websites and the internet than ever before. You know this. You are smart. That's why you are going to MAKE SURE you take advantage of this trend and utilize it to help grow your business. And that's why you will win. 💪

CHAPTER 4
WHY ARE YOU IN BUSINESS?

The *only* reason you're in business is to make money, right? WRONG! Over the last 20 years, people have really started thinking more about their passions and why they are getting into the type of business they're in. For those following their passion, it's pretty easy to find your "why." Simply ask yourself: what do you love about it? What about it excites you?

I've had hundreds of clients in the medical industry; from surgeons to doctors to nurses to hospitals. For those who chose it by their own free will, the answer is usually because they wanted to help people. Many of them had a family member or loved one suffer from a disease and wanted to do everything in their power to help others in the same situation.

THIS IS YOUR WHY.

I've also had the opportunity to work with hundreds in the legal industry: personal injury, criminal, employment, tax, and so on. Each of the people who chose their profession on their own volition will usually had a specific "why" too. One of my clients started his now multi-million dollar law firm because he wanted to help those looking for a better life. His family immigrated to the U.S. when he was young, and he saw how hard both of his parents worked to build a better life with more opportunities for him and his younger sister. He saw how his parents were taken advantage of in the US legal system because of the language barrier. This drove him to become one of the best immigration lawyers in the game today.

THIS IS YOUR WHY.

But not everyone had the luxury to choose their own profession by their own free will. Back in the day it was a little different. You got a job because you needed a job. You needed to help your family. You needed to put food on the table. There weren't as many opportunities as there are now. You were told by your parents to go to school and become a doctor, a lawyer, an accountant. To go work at a company and advance over the years. So how do you find your why?

One of my favorite quotes is "happiness is not in doing what one loves to do, but rather loving what one has to do." And it couldn't be more applicable here. In any business that you have, there is something you can find to love. I didn't grow up thinking my dream was to build websites and digital marketing campaigns for clients. What I did find was that I loved helping people, and I loved business, and I loved helping people build their businesses.

THIS IS YOUR WHY.

My family came from humble beginnings. As a kid, I always wished someone would give me some guidance, some mentorship, and the right answers to help me become successful. Over the years, I had some great mentors give me some incredible advice. Not everyone wanted to help, but oh how grateful I was to those that did. They helped train my mind to a higher level of thinking. The thinking that would both help me learn how to build, structure, and grow my business. I looked at these mentors like my heroes. I wanted to be like them. I wanted to help young kids like me trying to make a difference. I wanted to help single moms like my mom who would work 60+ hours a week. I wanted to help immigrant fathers like my dad who came here with limited understanding of the native language, legal system, and business environment. I wanted to help everyone who was willing to work. THIS IS MY WHY. THIS IS YOUR WHY.

WHY, WHAT, HOW

Your passion (why), your services (what), and your value (how)—this is what your potential clients care most about. This is what will entice them to want to work with you. And this is what you will put throughout your website to convert them from traffic, to new clients, to increased profitability for your business.

So how does this help your website? This is what develops your mission statement, your value proposition, and in turn the rest of the content for your website. Let's take this step-by-step and keep it easy.

MISSION STATEMENT

Exercise:

Go to:
www.EMRGonline.com/Powerhouse-Websites/my-mission-statement

On this page, we'll give you some guidance and tools to help create, further develop, or properly utilize your existing mission statement as part of your website.

Step 1

Think of why you decided to get into your business. What do you love about it? What motivates you to keep going?

Do you love helping people? Do you love defending or supporting people who aren't capable of doing it for themselves? Do you love the creativity that goes into your work? Do you love what you're able to provide for your customers/clients?

Are you motivated by being able to provide for your family? Are you motivated by keeping your employees paid to provide for their families?

Whatever reasons you can find, start writing it out.

Here are my reasons: I love helping people. I love empowering people through business and utilizing my experience to help them grow. I love being financially independent and utilizing my money to help people, while providing a comfortable life for myself and my loved ones.

Step 2

What does your company do? List out the services you provide.

Example: EMRG is a digital marketing and consulting firm.

Step 3

What's your value proposition? What makes you

different? Why should a customer/client choose you over a competitor?

Example: At EMRG, we have years of experience working across many different industries. Our specialty is all about conversions-focused websites, and data-driven digital marketing that help our clients increase their profitability.

Step 4

Now that you have your "why's", your company's offering, and your value proposition, you can work on compiling them into a few concise sentences to develop your mission statement.

Example:

Everything we do is for the sole purpose of having your company emerge online by increasing your growth, profitability, and presence to reach your online potential.

At EMRG, we look at ourselves as your partners throughout this process and ongoing relationship. We treat your business as it is our own, always with the intention of making the right decisions and using our experience to guide you towards further success.

We do this while keeping the highest levels of professionalism and integrity, and while incorporating GIVING BACK into our business model by sponsoring children in third world countries with each new campaign we launch.

Congratulations! You now have a working version of your mission statement to put on your website. I suggest including this on your "About" page, and possibly on your homepage as well. More importantly, this mission statement incorporates three vital elements that should structure the remainder of your website content, your branding through all digital avenues, and how you communicate with your client.

CHAPTER 5
BRANDING

One of the proudest moments of my career was at a conference a few years back. It was one of the first conferences my company and I attended to get some exposure for ourselves. We had done other kinds of marketing in the past (mostly digital—go figure) and wanted to get more publicity in some of the industries we had experience in. We had paid to have a booth to interact with some of the 15,000+ attendees. We set up some nice banners, monitors, brochures, and hand-outs with our logo and designs. My mindset going into this was to meet as many people as possible and make them aware of our digital marketing firm, EMRG (officially pronounced Emerge, though many still call us E.M.R.G.). What I didn't know was just how much all the previous work I did was going to help me here.

On the first day, I vividly recall an attendee coming by our booth to pick up one of our brochures just minutes before the vendor exhibits opened. He was well-dressed in a nice suit and shirt, but without a tie. He looked about 45 years old and carried himself well, but he was moving quickly. I approached politely, introduced myself, and started to talk a bit about who we were and what we did. Before I could even begin he said, "Ya ya ya, I know who you guys are. We'll chat later." He nodded his head several times and left in a flurry. Damn, that was cold. My first rejection of the day. He obviously didn't have any intention of coming back. How would he know who we were? Did he work at the event, or was he just trying to get away? All good, on to the next one. I've been in business long enough to know not to let this get to me. Plus, I had some of my staff here with me. I needed to put on a strong face and gather some enthusiasm to lead by example.

A minute later, another attendee came to our booth and excitedly cheered, "Hey Team Emerge!" She was a sweet woman. And she got our acronym pronounced right too. She started telling us how she was looking for our booth once she heard we were at the event. Apparently, she had seen our work before and was interested in learning more.

She heard about us?! She knew who we were? She knew our work? She knew how to pronounce our company name? I was so ecstatic to hear that. We were still a relatively small firm at this point, so to hear anybody "knows about us" is exciting. It was like the first taste of semi-fame. I needed to find out all the details about this.

I had a chance to speak with her for a bit. She was super friendly and excited to hear more about us. Without wanting to seem surprised at her recognition of her company, I attempted to nonchalantly ask, "I appreciate the nice words, but I have to ask. How did you hear about us? Where did you see our work?" She told me that she had seen a website we had created in her industry. Our company info is at the bottom of that site, and from there she did some digging on our website. She was really impressed with our designs and had thought of reaching out to us a few months prior, but got busy with work. While reviewing one of the "welcome" emails she got about this event, she saw our logo and immediately recognized us! She decided to schedule the first 10 minutes of the vendor exhibit hall to chat with us to build her company's website. I can't explain how happy this made me. All these years of hard work and people now recognize us and our talent. This isn't even THE proud moment I was talking about.

To make things even better, our booth had about 8 people hovering around waiting to speak with us within minutes. I heard some similar stories of people who had seen some of our social content, best practices, other websites, other designs, and even a few referrals. The rest of the event was just as great. We were constantly meeting new people, being approached by some that already knew about us, and doing our best to keep up with the demand. But the best part was still to come.

Remember that first guy who rejected me before I even had a chance to speak? He came back on the last day. I shot him a smile and a nod as he was walking towards our booth to be polite since we recognized each other. I realized he was coming back to our table. "Sorry, I didn't get a chance to chat last time. I've been meaning to come back and chat to learn more about you guys. I've seen your ads a dozen times and have seen your videos in the past. I like your approach about utilizing a website to grow profits. My office desperately needs a new website and someone to guide us on what we should be doing. How do we get started?"

I didn't even bring contracts to this event! I didn't think we'd get this response. I didn't know people knew us. I didn't think people would recognize us. There was a big lesson here that hit me like a lightning bolt and stayed with me forever: **branding builds recognition**.

Several of these people saw our videos, saw our previous websites, and saw our designs. But they recognized us because of our company name. They recognized our logo. They recognized our content, our verbiage, our value proposition, and mission statement. They recognized our company colors. The image was memorable, and gave them a specific impression of us. An almost engineered impression that we wanted them to have. This is branding. These are the benefits of brandings.

Branding is a combination of design aesthetics and your mission statement as a message through the impression you're communicating. Read that again. Design aesthetics can include things like fonts, styles, tonality, designs, colors, shapes, etc. And your mission statement is the message that your brand is trying to communicate through your content and design. Branding incorporates both design and your mission, and leaves an impression on your audience. Branding creates your identity and helps your audience identify and distinguish your company from others.

Your branding design should evoke certain feelings in your viewers. For EMRG, we wanted to showcase that we are a professional, experienced, and tech-based company. We wanted to display our business acumen. We wanted to illustrate our design and creative talents. That's why when we updated our website, we chose to use a combination of modern-techy fonts, a minimalist design, along with image-centric displays of our past website work. We included case studies and analytics to show off the results.

When attendees saw our booth at the conference they recognized our booth's backdrop design that included our logo, our fonts, our color scheme, and our company name. An important factor to remember was that this wasn't their first time seeing us. They had seen our website before with our mission statement. They had seen our work before. If your branding is how memorable you are, then the quality of the memory depends on your past work and reputation. If you've performed well in the past, you've further established a positive memorable impression. This can go the other way too, which is why it's imperative for your success to always act in good faith and with strong morals.

"Your reputation is like your virginity. You can only lose it once!"

Lastly, it's important to realize that, for many attendees at the conference, this was the first time they saw EMRG. You can't expect everyone to remember your brand the first time they encounter it or you. Repetitive exposure to your brand will help it become memorable, as will the depth of the interaction someone has with your brand. Meeting someone in person and having a meaningful conversation where you can provide value to someone will have a more lasting effect than a quick email. Multiple interactions will have a deeper impact than just one. A combination of these will probably serve you and your brand best.

Let's put what you learned into action. Use the following link to help guide you through a quick activity to further develop or create your brand: www.EMRGonline.com/Powerhouse-Websites/develop-my-brand

1. An effective brand communicates a specific message, is in line with your mission, and gives your audience a specific impression of who you are. Jot down any keywords or feelings that you want people to perceive when seeing your brand. Reference your mission statement and value proposition to ensure you're communicating the right message.

2. Pick your style: find 3 designs or brands that reflect the design you envision for your brand. These can be any designs and are not limited to companies nor your industry.

3. Write what specifically about these designs you like as articulately as possible.

Check you out! You're now further establishing your branding! You should be very proud of yourself. Most people go through their whole lives without understanding these concepts. This base for your branding will now serve as the design and messaging you'll use throughout all of your media: website, digital, social, print, verbal, and anything else you can think of.

CHAPTER 6
IDENTIFYING YOUR TARGET

By now you've heard me say a few times to **start with the end goal in mind.** We know what our end goal is. Now it's time to shift gears but apply the same principle: who is our end customer? During this chapter you'll figure out who your target audience is and hone in on them using design and your website.

Scenario 1

You already have a business. You may or may not have already noticed a trend in your customers: who they are, where they live, their age, their gender, their personality type, their buying habits, and as many details as you can think of. If not, it's time to start thinking of this. By understanding your current target audience, you can custom tailor your messaging, your tonality, your design, and all else to better align with them.

Scenario 2

You are just starting your business. You might not be entirely sure who your exact target audience is, but with some critical thinking, you will have some ideas of who your market consists of. The best thing for you to do is to start testing your different potential markets and follow the data to see who your actual target market is. After some time, you'll get a clear picture of the market(s) that respond best to your product/service offerings, and you can now focus on this market.

I'll share a couple examples of some of my clients and how we use our understanding of their respective markets to really help propel their business growth. One of our clients is a top personal injury law firm in the country. They are headed by some extremely competent and experienced lawyers and have a large legal staff. Their office is immaculate—beautiful views in a high-end location, glass conference rooms, the works. Early on, we noticed that a large percentage of their clients only spoke Spanish. This was a bit unique because none of their partners or lawyers were of Hispanic descent, and the area they were located in was not primarily Spanish-speaking. To make it even more interesting, they never noticed how much of their audience were Hispanic and had not spent a dollar on any Hispanic-targeted marketing... yet.

This specific demographic was their target market. We knew it right off the bat. A few discussions with the partners later, and I explained to them the benefit of having a Spanish-translation function on the website and running some digital marketing towards more of this specific demographic. We did so well with website conversions/leads coming in that the partners ended up hiring more Spanish-speaking staff to both onboard these new clients and help manage these cases to keep up with the workload.

Let me give you an example of another client. Let's call him Client X. Client X is a bit cooler than most. You'll never catch him in a suit—because he's on a surfboard, hoverboard, or electric bike most of the time. Those are the products he sells too. If you check his website out, one of the first things you'll notice is the tonality of his content. While a law firm's website typically represents them as professional, cordial, and corporate, Client X is more of a wild child. His content is a lot more casual, and it makes perfect sense because his customers are all a bit more 'chill.' They're looking for someone who speaks their language. He's a thrill seeker, and that resonates with his target demographic. Surfers, boarders, adrenaline junkies, and adventure seekers love the edgy designs and branding. We use this unique and authentic branding across the website, the social platforms, and the email marketing. Because of that, they resonate with his brand and his company, then buy more of his products. They don't think of any other company when it comes to these types of products. Why? Because his clients feel they BELONG to his brand and vice versa. They understand each other. They're of the same tribe.

So, you have some new tools now to add to your arsenal, building your business with each chapter and each step from this book. You learned how important it is to have a deep understanding of your target demographic. Knowledge is power, especially when it's about your specific target audience. When you know who your audience is, you know what they like to see, where they're looking, and possibly what designs will resonate with them.

I also know my target audience. I know the people actually reading this book are the go-getters. You are the people who aren't just here to learn about best website practices and growing your business—you are the action-takers. You take initiative and want to implement what you learn here. You are MY kind of people, and I am yours. Something that's been really helpful for me is to take notes and put things into action right after I learn it. This is why I've created some quick activities at each step of this book to help you organize and build on your thoughts. I know that you're probably busy in life too, so I built out our exercises in a way to continuously show you the notes you've already taken, and to help organize your thoughts so by the end of this process you have a strong outline of the future of your website (and possibly your business).

Go to the following link to help you further discover your target demographic and how you can cater to them more closely:
www.EMRGonline.com/Powerhouse-Websites/target-demographic

For the following exercise, use your existing customer/client-base to answer the following questions. Identify up to 3 of your largest audiences if applicable.

If you're a relatively new business, make some educated guesses as to who you think your target demographics include and come back to this exercise as your customer-base grows.

1. Is your target audience male, female, or a mix? If a mix, what percentage each?

2. What is their typical age range?

3. What is their education level?

4. What do you think their income range is?

5. Briefly describe any similarities you've found in their personalities/behaviors.

6. What tonality do they speak in? What tonality do they want you to speak?

7. What designs and colors resonate with your audience?

CHAPTER 7
DESIGN

Design is one of the most important topics when talking about your website. But there are so many details and areas to cover. People study design for decades. For the purpose of your website, we're going to break down the most important design principles and equip you with some tools to help you along your mission, utilizing your website and all the steps we have learned earlier on.

I've had a chance to personally be a part of 5000+ website projects, spanning from local mom-and-pops to multinational multi-billion dollar firms. I've worked across dozens of industries, from legal to leisure, medical to manufacturing, and everything in between. As different as these industries are, my team and I were able to accumulate enough data over the past 20 years to identify recurring design elements that led to success. And, I'm opening my playbook for you to use to help you grow your business and hopefully achieve your life goals.

Here are the design elements that the great, high-performing and conversion-focused websites have:

MINIMALISM

Less is more. The last thing you want to do is overcrowd your website by having too much information. Nothing gets seen this way. Too much content looks like a newspaper. Your potential clients are not coming on to your website to read a newspaper though. Their attention span is short. Very short in fact. You have 5 seconds at most to capture their attention and have them find what they're looking for. This is why it's important to have good organization with titles, subtitles, and a nice page-balance of text and images.

It's important to keep a nice balance between imagery and content. Too many images can even crowd a page. Having some space between sections will help visitors absorb the vital information that you are trying to communicate. Imagine 5 people in a small room yelling at you all at once. No matter how loud they all yell, you won't hear anything. Conversely, if you have one person distinctly say one thing at a time in that room, even without yelling, you will hear it loud and clear.

Moreover, if this one person is yelling the entire time they talk you will slowly start ignoring them. THAT'S WHY YOU DON'T WRITE THE ENTIRE WEBSITE IN CAPS. You use it sparingly. You use it to communicate only certain points. While titles, subtitles, **bold,** and sometimes even using the <u>underline</u> functionality can be useful, using any of these too often will congest your page. This is why the use of minimalism is so powerful. When it comes to your website,

one **POWERFUL** word

in black ink on a white canvas can leave more of an impact and have more power than an encyclopedia filled with colorful information.

DRIVING CONVERSIONS/CALL-TO-ACTIONS

Okay, so now you have a simple website integrating minimalism. You have that powerful word in black ink on the white canvas. What does that word say? This is where you incorporate your value messaging from the earlier chapter to communicate the benefits to your client, and utilize **call-to-actions** on your website to trigger your visitors to **convert!** The entire purpose of your website is to get your website visitors to convert into online sales, appointments, patients, clients, or donors. This is where you do it. You've created a beautiful website with a minimalist design and a strong message portraying the value they will receive. Now you give them the opportunity to work with you so you can provide them this benefit.

Call-to-actions come in all shapes and sizes. If you're a medical office or surgical center, you want to offer options for prospective patients to fill out contact forms, call the number on your website directly to schedule, or even fill out a "schedule appointment" calendar function. As an e-commerce business, the ultimate call-to-action would be for your visitor to make an online purchase. Call-to-actions are unique to each industry and can/should be unique to your specific business process. Make this easy for you and your new client by including your call-to-action at the end of every page. Make sure they can find it everywhere on the site so they are always just one click away from getting to you.

USER EXPERIENCE (UX) & USER INTERFACE (UI)

Making it easier on a website visitor to find what they're looking for will evoke more people to take action. Read that again. If you make it easy on them, they are more likely to do it. So logically our next question is 'how do we make it easy?' Through great **UX and UI**.

UX stands for user experience. It is the process, emotions, and effortlessness the user experiences when navigating your website. A good UX is fun, easy, simple, and intuitive. Think of a great tech product you bought at any point in your life. I personally remember the flat screen 65-inch TV I got a few years ago. What a great day. A fantastic product, and super easy to use. I took it out of the box, plugged it into the outlet and cable, and pressed the power button on the remote. I pressed the "menu" button to find what I was looking for, and easily navigated with the channel and volume buttons. Everything was where I expected it to be. My UX was perfect.

UI stands for user interface. It is the structure of the design when navigating and utilizing functions. For my TV, the menu button was large and centered on my remote—when I clicked it I was taken to several options, each with submenus contained within them. Easy peasy.

Your website should have the same effects. Don't get caught up with being flashy. You want people to come to your website and easily find what they are looking for. Don't forget, you have 5 seconds max, and that's being generous. Your menu should be easy to navigate, and people should enjoy the process of finding what they're looking for.

Apple is a great example of a company with a great UX and UI. They created their systems to be as intuitive as possible based on human behavior. They've made their operating systems simple, minimalistic, and fun to use. This is why their products have had such huge success. Most people don't have the time nor patience to try and figure out how to use/navigate through a difficult website. This is the same reason why your website can have great success with your visitors if you do a good job.

Here are a few easy examples to illustrate:

- Someone is in need of your services. They enter your website and immediately see your contact number on the header of all your pages on your website. They can easily pick up the phone and hire you.

- Someone enters your e-commerce website. By having a quick link on your homepage with a few of your best selling products, you are immediately offering an opportunity for someone to add a product to your cart, ultimately leading to a sale.

But not all platforms or devices are created equal. This adds some variables that we need to prepare for in order to be successful across the board.

MOBILE AND RESPONSIVE

In 2003, only 16.2% of all web traffic worldwide was through mobile. In 2021 that number shot up to 56%.[1] That means more than half of your potential visitors are on mobile devices, and you can see where the trend is heading. For some businesses this number is even higher! Yes, you have to make sure your website is 100% mobile-friendly. It has to be just as easy to use on a smartphone as it is on a desktop. This requires strategy, because the same principles we discussed earlier apply. Except now you have a much smaller canvas to get your message across.

Mobile is not the only other type of device you need to adjust for. There are tablets, large desktop monitors, TV displays, projectors, and probably dozens of others. It's vital for your website to be built as **responsive**. A responsive website means that your website adjusts to the device it is being displayed on (it RESPONDS to the device it's being viewed on). The website recognizes if it is on a desktop monitor and displays in its full glory. It also identifies if it is being opened on a tablet, smaller device, larger device, or mobile device and acts accordingly. Word to the wise though: having your website built to be responsive is not enough. You need to run quality assurance tests across each platform, with each page, and each

---

1. Information obtained from https://www.broadband-search.net/blog/mobile-desktop-internet-usage-statistics

function to guarantee it. That's just part of what goes into a great website.

If you're unsure or need some help reviewing your website's responsiveness, use our free tool: www.EMRGonline.com/Powerhouse-Websites/ mobile-friendly-and-responsive-website-test

CHAPTER 8
FUNCTIONALITY

Let me tell you guys about a story with one of my clients. Let's call him Client O. Client O was a very particular person. He's extremely intelligent, very picky, and meticulously organized. Some would say he has major OCD (hence Client "O"). I would definitely be one of those people. He was a nice guy though. I liked his style, his way of thinking, and he's been extremely successful arguably because of it.

Client O had a habit of overthinking, including when it came to his website. He had a detailed diagram of exactly how he wanted everything to work. He had the overall design sketched based on what he researched would work well, he had a multi-step process for the functionality when users would come on his website, and he had another multi-step process for his users to follow to automate his business processes. This is just the tip of the iceberg. I will spare you all the different nuances and other functionality he had planned out when he handed a binder of 50+ pages.

While his detailed plan of action was well thought-out, complexity ended up being his biggest obstacle. Although everything seemed logical to him (despite how many times we suggested a simpler version), his plan made many assumptions about user behavior and what to expect from his website traffic. His website ended up being an intelligent algorithm of functions and processes... that never caught traction. Users were not as eager to learn and go through his system as he had thought. Quite simply, it was not simple enough.

Think of Amazon.com. Amazon has a ton of products, tons of categories, and a ton of subcategories. But they organized things in a way to be as easy and intuitive as possible. This way you find what you're looking for quickly and can spend money on the site (conversion). To make things even easier, Amazon added a "buy it now" button for one-click checkout, removing the need to even add to cart, review, then to check out. Why wouldn't they? The less steps you have to take to make a purchase, the more likely you are to follow through on your purchase. They utilized functionality to make things easier for their audience while pushing for their goal: a purchase or conversion.

Another great example of smart functionality is Dominos.com. I love their website: super easy to use, mobile-friendly, large images to make it easy to understand and follow along, and you can view toppings on the picture as you add them to your pizza. This makes the experience easy and fun. But the genius behind their functionality is not just the animated toppings. It's the checkout. When you are about to checkout, they have a quick pop-up that offers you a 2 liter coke. Imagine how many people add this on to their order. Where they get me is the next pop-up: brownies, cinnamon rolls, and all other kinds of desserts. Smart move Dominos, presenting me with a call-to-action in as easy a fashion as possible. Now I have to burn off these extra calories...

Let's think about your website. Think of your goal and what call-to-action you want visitors to take. Think of what will help with your UX and UI, simplify the process for your visitors, and make things more convenient for them at the same time. There are unlimited possibilities here, but I've shared 10 easy and effective functionalities we've seen implemented on websites across all industries:

1. Livechat - Allow potential customers to chat with your company immediately during working hours. We've set this up to many of our clients' cell phones, allowing them to answer it like they would a text message in real-time and capture a new client.

2. Schedule An Appointment - For most service based businesses, this is the easiest way to have an initial meeting or appointment with a prospective client.

3. Prepayment For Services - For those offering services, you can have people prepay and purchase hours, packages, or gift cards directly through your site and schedule with you after.

4. Customized Forms - You can custom-tailor forms specific to your industry and business to help you get the process started with a new or returning client. Easy and effective.

5. File Upload - For businesses that require a client to provide some documentation in order to begin services, you can have a file upload functionality to allow a website visitor to upload the file directly to your website, notifying you in real-time.

6. Customized Social Media Links - You can get creative here. If you have any prominent social platforms that you want to promote or even showcase, there are ways to integrate this with your site to make it captivating and add design to your website.

7. Blogs/Events/In The News - While all of these work through blog functionality, you can essentially use this format to continuously post new pieces of content chronologically for website visitors to keep up with your company activities.

8. Newsletter Sign-Up - Capturing email addresses (especially with a quick pop-up when people first enter the site) is an easy way to stay in touch with potential clients who might not be ready to follow-through on a call-to-action just yet.

9. Integrated Google Map - This is especially effective for local businesses who have people drive to their location. This should be placed on your contact page, as well as on your footer for quick access—especially if people are using your website to get directions on their phone when coming to your business.

10. User Logins - Depending on your type of business, this can be a make-it or break-it functionality. For any business that runs through your website (e-commerce, online education, online dating, etc) you MUST make the login section feel like home. Again, Amazon is a great example. You can quickly view your orders, your cart, your wishlist, and more. This is easy and comfortable for people who come back regularly. There's no place like home.

CHAPTER 9
CONTENT

DO I HAVE YOUR ATTENTION?

TITLES & TAGLINES

If you're on this page then my large title likely caught your attention. Titles and taglines can be simple and effective when used sparingly on each page. And you can entice readers to continue reading; especially if it's relevant to what they're looking for. Your goal is to capture and captivate. But it can't just be large print alone. If you write a paragraph in a super large-sized font, everything will get drowned out (Google Einstein's Theory of Relativity if you don't believe me). The key to successful titles and taglines is to keep things CRISP:

CRISP

Concise

Relevant

Interesting

Sharp

Powerful

Imagine this: you now have all your ideal pages. You have an easy-to-understand layout, simplistic and beautiful design with a strong sense of branding. Your functionality is immaculate; it serves your goals, and helps your audience. You have all these pages and functions on your website, but what do you fill in the pages with?

There's an expression in our industry that most people (including those in our industry) still don't know. CONTENT IS KING. Great content is the x-factor, the differentiator between someone coming to your website and browsing vs. someone coming to your website and knowing they **must** work with your company. But what takes your content from just existing to good. And even more difficult, how do you take your content from good to GREAT?

Early on we spoke about your mission statement and the value you offer your clients. There was a reason that this was the driving force behind your entire website. It wasn't just meant for your titles, design, and functionality. This should be at the core of your content and how you communicate to your clients through your website—as well as **all other** communication.

AUTHENTIC VOICE

The style and tonality of your content should be reflective of how you speak to your clients. In a corporate setting, tonality tends to be more professional and cordial. In a more creative environment there tends to be more flexibility.

I've seen outliers on both sides. Ultimately it depends on your audience and how you run your business. Whatever your style is, use it in your content on your website, digital, and even print to keep your branding and communication cohesive across all channels.

If you are a manufacturer of home goods, you can easily write "we manufacture home goods" on your website and easily list out all our categories and products. This content just exists. But if you write "we handcraft home goods using the highest quality materials," you are showing more of the value you offer versus competitors. Your content went from existing to good.

Now, imagine you wrote "with over 20+ years of experience in the industry, we use our expertise to provide you with the highest quality products to turn your house into a home." Now you've gone from good to great. It's not about writing more. Yes, you want depth, but too much content will overwhelm readers and they'll end up not reading any of it. There's a formula to success here that you can apply to any business to make your content great.

INCORPORATING YOUR MISSION AND VALUE

First, remember your mission statement. This is what your goal is as a business. Remind yourself of your mission and include this in your content as it relates to your products or services. Next, think of your value proposition. What benefit are you offering your clients? In the previous example we mentioned home goods. The benefits of these home goods might include the health safeguards that higher quality materials offer. Going a bit deeper, these higher quality materials might keep a family safe from toxins when serving food in them regularly. THAT's the benefit and value to your customers, not the products themselves.

Let's think about my company, EMRG. Yes, we provide digital marketing consulting and services: Websites, SEO, Ads Management, Social Media, Email Marketing, Online Reputation Management, and a host of others. But the benefit we offer our clients is the growth they get from our services. Our clients get to see their businesses grow and ultimately increase profitability when working with us. Our clients get to actualize their dreams of their entrepreneurial and business journey. So this is what we talk about on our website.

This is what makes our company different from competitors. This is what we focus on as a team internally everyday as we come into work. This is why we build our processes and strategies the way we do. Therefore, this is what we communicate to our clients. And, we practice what I'm preaching: we incorporate our mission statement too.

Everything we do is for the sole purpose of having your company emerge online by increasing your growth, profitability, and presence to reach your online potential, while incorporating Giving Back into our business model.

VISUALIZE SPEAKING WITH YOUR CLIENT

But how do we put this into writing? Sometimes it's difficult to put your value down with pen and paper (keyboard and computer would be more fitting). The reality of it is you already have this knowledge, you just need to access it. Imagine you have a potential client sitting in front of you or on the phone (whatever is more typical for your business). They ask you "why should I work with your company?" What's your response?

Your response is exactly what they are look-ing for. It is the value you offer your clients. It's what makes your company different from your competitors. What you do uniquely at your business. It's the benefits you are able to offer your clients through your experience, expertise, services, products, and all else. In other words, your value proposition.

It is driven by why you are in business: your mission statement.

CHAPTER 10
SEO

SEO has been a very sexy term in digital marketing for the past 10 years, but most people don't know what it is. SEO stands for Search Engine Optimization. Let's break this down further. Search engines are places on the internet where you search for things; like Google, Bing, Yahoo (for the few who still use it), etc. To "optimize" on one of these search engines, this implies that you are optimizing your website. But how do you optimize your website on a search engine, and what's the purpose of doing this?

Let's start with the end-goal of SEO. If you optimize your website correctly you will have traffic directed to your website from these search engines when people search for specific keywords that are related to your business's offerings (as listed on your website). Here's an easy example: suppose your company provides cosmetic surgery; specifically, hair restoration surgery to those with receding hairlines or balding. A prospective patient will search the internet for "hair surgeon near me," or "best hair surgeon." If you have strong SEO marketing backing your website, you can have your website show up first on Google when someone searches Google for these terms. Being in the top spot as a search result for these highly sought-after keywords, you will get a majority of the people searching these terms to your website. If you have a well-built and conversion-focused website (see chapters 1-9), these website visitors turn into paying patients. This applies to any industry by understanding the keywords that are related to yours.

Undoubtedly, your competitors will try to compete for this #1 position too. So, how do you optimize your website to show up ahead of theirs? SEO encompasses a lot. I can write an entirely separate book just on the best strategies and concepts specific to SEO (a possible indication of what's to come from my desk in the future). I've spoken about SEO in front of thousands and across dozens of industries. The same principles apply across the board as they all relate to what these search engines are looking for when ranking different websites. Typically if I'm giving a keynote presentation on SEO I'm spending about two hours minimum, going into depth on each section with examples. That's not my purpose here. My purpose is to give you a macro-understanding of what SEO is and the main principles that constitute what's involved in a great SEO strategy. Here we go:

1. Keyword Strategy

The starting point of your SEO journey should begin with your keyword strategy. This involves a combination of your service/product offerings and should focus on what is most profitable for your business while taking into consideration the competition levels of each of these keywords. From our experience, I can tell you that you don't always need the most sought-after keyword to be successful. Something with enough search volume (possibly something niche) can be a lot easier to rank for and bring you a ton of profits.

Example: "Personal Injury Law Firm" is a target keyword.

2. Website Content

Now that you know what keywords you're looking to target, the content on your website should reflect it. By targeting these search terms with your content, search engine bots are more likely to perceive your pages as more relevant to these respective keywords, and therefore rank you higher for them when people search. Back in the day you used to see a keyword repeated hundreds of times on a given webpage to manipulate rankings. This doesn't work anymore. The search engines have smartened, and so should you. Keep it natural, keep it original (they penalize you for duplicate content), and keep it in-line with the brand message. You still have visitors coming to your site that need to see what you're about.

Example: Page on your website titled "The XXXXX Personal Injury Law Firm," with content on that page that incorporates "personal injury law firm" within the content several times.

3. Website On-Page Optimization

Now that you have your keywords chosen and have written content to be specific to them, you need to optimize the pages on your website. By having things like page titles created to be as close to your selected keywords as possible, you're helping search engine bots index each of your pages (along with the content that sits on those pages) to rank. Titles are just the tip of the iceberg; here's a short-list of some other items that are included in the on-page optimization we include when we launch a SEO campaign. These can be quite technical and overwhelming, but I want to make you aware of them in the larger scope of SEO. A quick Google search will explain each with easy examples:

- Proper Sitemap
- Anchor Text
- Meta Tags
- H1 Tags
- Alt Tags
- Keyword Density
- Content Structure

4. Content and Backlinks

While getting your website optimized is a strong starting point, it's only the starting point. SEO can be extremely competitive. If you want to win you have to continuously create fresh content both on your website and externally. You can create fresh content on your website by including things like a blog, where you can update regularly or by adding new pages to your website often (as long as they follow the structure given earlier).

External content gets a bit trickier. You now have to coordinate with third party sites, often paying-to-play. But you can't just post content to any website. Your goal is to post on reputable and high-quality websites (as perceived by the search engine). For example, if you were to get your article featured on a major news publication's website you would gain a lot more juice than by having your cousin Ernie post your article on his rock collection website that only gets viewed by him (and now you).

Assuming you did get on a credible website with relative content, what's next? How does a search engine create a connection from this website to your website? Through backlinking. By having a part of the content (preferably your target keyword) on the third party website link directly back to your website (preferably the page you have targeting that keyword), you're now implicating your webpage to be ranked for that specific keyword.

Example: Imagine that a large news publication has written an article about your law firm, and within the article, they've used the keyword "personal injury law firm," with a hyperlink from that keyword directly to the page on your website that you also title "personal injury law firm." Presto! A promising backlink.

Now do this 100 times…. every month… consistently… until you're top ranked. Then rinse and repeat. If you decide to stop, after some time you'll notice your rankings will slip to other more active competitors. While I think it's a great strategy to do as much of the SEO basics as early on as possible, I am constantly urging my clients who ask for us to run their SEO to make sure they can afford it indefinitely. It can and has been extremely profitable for many of my clients, but only those who were willing to stick it out. SEO is a long-term strategy. Just like anything else, if you want to be successful with it, you have to commit.

FINAL NOTES

I hope you enjoyed this book. If I was able to help you or your business even slightly, then it was worth all the long nights of thinking, writing, and editing. We are all on this journey called Life together. I try my best to always practice kindness and generosity; I've shared all of my years of experience in as concise a format as possible to hopefully save you some of the headaches and tough lessons I had to learn first-hand.

I do enjoy business, very much, in fact. A big part of why I love it is because it acts as a tool allowing me to help others in the many ways I plan to.

When I leave the world I hope I leave a positive impact—for my loving family, my amazing team, and all of you incredible people out there.

If you need any help along your digital marketing journey, feel free to reach out to us at info@EMRGonline.com. We will do our best to help as many of you as we can.

ACKNOWLEDGEMENTS

First and foremost, I'd like to thank my family.

Mom, thank you for teaching me about work ethic through example, and giving me the tools of self-improvement. Seeing you work so hard for us was what lit the fire of my ambition in life.

Dad, thank you for always teaching me to think big, to be a leader, and to pursue greatness.

My grandmother Mommy Farokh and late grandfather Papa, you both made such a large impact on the person I became through the love and time you gave me.

My sister Amanda and brother-in-law Alan, thank you for always wanting what's best for me.

My cousins and all my other family, all the lessons and love you have given me have helped me get to this part of my life.

My work family, I would not be here without you. Thank you for believing in me (and putting up with me). Thank you for all your hard work, all of your loyalty and honesty. Thank you for demanding the best of yourself everyday, and in turn, the best of me. You all inspire me greatly and are a big reason I will continue to work hard. We still have some big goals and celebrations ahead of us, and I'm excited to be on this journey with you.

My best friends and brothers (you all know who you are). You have seen me at my best and my worst, and have stuck with me throughout. You have always been there when I needed help, and I'll never forget that. To many more years of friendship and brotherhood.

Josh, thank you for editing this book for me and lending me your incredible writing skills. Thank you for helping me find my voice, and ensuring my writing style was authentic and cohesive.

Michael, thank you for your tireless review of this book many times over. Without your help, this book would have been a mess of words and incorrect punctuation.

To my mentors, thank you for always believing in me. Thank you for showing me the right path when it was not always visible to me. Thank you for always being so humble and giving me the credit at a milestone, even though you helped pave the way.

Bobby, your continuous lessons and support helped shape my way of thinking, and consequently, who I am and how I live my life.

Patrick, your entrepreneurial teaching and principles, along with your continued support years after my education at USC, have been monumental for me.

To all my readers, thank you for picking up this book and investing in yourself. Life is a beautiful journey with continuous lessons. I hope you enjoyed this book!

Made in the USA
Las Vegas, NV
18 September 2023

77780558R00066